SUMMARY

Never Split
The Difference

Chris Voss & Tahl Raz!

*Negotiating As If
Your Life Depended On It*

Speed-Summary

Before we proceed...

Feel free to follow us on social media to learn success lessons from successful people, and investment opportunities.

Instagram: @Investor_Valley

https://www.instagram.com/investor_valley

TABLE OF CONTENTS

Introduction

Never Split the Difference is a book written by Chris Voss and Tahl Raz. Voss works as a professor of negotiation at the University in Southern California Marshall School of Business and the Georgetown University McDonough School of Business, while Raz has already co-authored several books on leadership and business achievement together with Keith Ferrazzi and Gary Burnison. Raz also writes for many publications, including the Wall Street Journal and the New York Times. Never Split the Difference is a book about negotiations.

Negotiations take place in many different fields of life, such as business, and in some critical situations, like hostage situations. The book is actually a guide on how to best behave when certain things happen, regardless of whether that includes the need for negotiation techniques in hostage situations or in business. Throughout the book, the authors describe what to do, what kind of questions to ask, and how to react in a situation that requires negotiation. These techniques include active listening, assertive speech, knowing how to remain calm despite the situation, and much more.

Definitely a book that can teach its readers something new and useful, Never Split the Difference is a guide for both beginners and those who consider themselves to be experts at negotiation. It offers new perspectives that will help to improve anyone's negotiations skills.

Chapter 1: The New Rules | How to Become the Smartest Person...in Any Room

Chris Voss begins by explaining he's been in the FBI for more than 20 years, which includes 15 years negotiating hostage situations around the world. During this time, he was the only lead international kidnapping negotiator in the Bureau. Negotiating has been a fundamental part of his job and he describes how this experience has influenced everything in his life from dealing with customer service representatives to parenting. FBI negotiating techniques are built from observational learning, by sharing what works and what doesn't out in the field. They are effective for all kinds of human interactions.

He describes a story of when he taking an executive negotiation course at Harvard Law School to learn more about negotiating from a business point of view. He was invited to a meeting with two expert negotiators - Robert Mnookin, a Harvard law professor and expert in conflict resolution, and Gabriella Blum, a specialist in international negotiations, armed conflict, and counterterrorism. They put Voss on the spot by role-playing a hostage situation where they had captured his son. They were requesting $1 million in exchange for his life.

Voss responded with a powerful FBI tool - the open-ended question. He refers to this as 'tactical calibrated questions,' which allows the other side to respond yet there are no fixed answers. It has several benefits. It buys you time and gives your counterpart the illusion of control. At the same time, it constrains them without them even realizing it.

During the role-play, every threat to his son was deflected by Voss asking how he was supposed to know his son was alive and how he was supposed to pay Mnookin. In the end, Mnookin and Blum were unable to steer the conversation beyond Voss's demands and they gave up.

Voss explains that the negotiation techniques at Harvard are based on mathematical logic. However, real-life negotiations are never straightforward. They are irrational, impulsive, and emotionally driven. We react based on our deepest fears, needs, desires, and perceptions. It makes negotiating unpredictable and complex and it can't be reduced to a neat script or a sequence of actions and offers.

He describes two schools of thoughts for negotiating. The first is the rational problem solving at Harvard. This aims to overcome the emotional brain with a rational mindset. It assumes that both negotiating parties are ready to problem-solve together and want to reach a mutually beneficial deal. The second (used by the FBI) believes negotiating is based on psychology, counseling, and crisis intervention. It uses research that concludes that the human mind is irrational and "feeling" is an important form of thinking. It contrasts to the Harvard idea that believes humans are rational actors.

Research by Daniel Kahneman identifies two systems of thought in the brain. System one is the emotional, animal, and instinctive part and it acts quickly to external demands. System two is the slow and logical part. It is strongly - yet unconsciously - influenced by system one. Negotiators need to communicate with system one as negotiations are not rational, problem-solving situations. Instead, they are charged with emotions. Feelings and emotions, therefore, are central to effective negotiations.

People want to be understood and accepted. By listening intensely, it shows empathy and a desire to better understand what the other side is experiencing. People are less defensive and oppositional when they feel listened to and are more likely to listen to the other side's view. It also moves the person into a calm and logical place. Voss refers this as 'tactical empathy'. Tactical empathy is critical in negotiations.

Negotiating, according to Voss, is not about gradually weakening or destroying the other side. It's about playing an emotional game in order to get what you want by asking in the correct way. By learning to better understand emotions, you can better connect and influence others and ultimately, achieve more. This is critical in the role of a hostage negotiator, as they must walk away with everything they ask for.

Chapter 2: Be a Mirror | How to Quickly Establish Rapport

Voss begins the chapter by describing his first proper hostage situation. Armed robbers had taken hostages at a bank and tensions were high. The New York Police Department, SWAT, and FBI were all outside prepared to attack if necessary. The police had arrived assuming it would all be over quickly as they had been told the robbers wanted to surrender. However, they had been fed false information. The police were communicating with one robber inside the bank who was relaying all sorts of information to further confuse them while giving himself more time to think of an escape route.

It took hours of careful negotiation, yet eventually, the robbers released the hostages and surrendered. This hostage situation encompassed some key negotiation skills.

Voss says negotiators should arrive at the negotiation without assumptions. Assumptions can paint a fixed and possibly flawed version of the situation. Instead, the negotiator should hold several hypotheses in mind at the same time that could possibly explain what's going on. As the negotiation continues, all new information that comes from the exchange can be used to test and separate the true hypotheses from the false ones. Voss stresses that a good negotiator questions assumptions and remains emotionally open to all possibilities.

During the negotiations with the armed bank robbers, Voss worked alongside another negotiator. He says that all negotiators work with someone as it provides an extra pair of ears and eyes to pick up subtle clues. Listening is one of the most important parts of negotiating, yet it's not easy. It's common to participate in "selective listening" where we only hear what we want to hear. This is due to cognitive bias, where our brains seek consistency with our assumptions, rather than looking for the truth.

Another common problem with listening is that people end up listening to the voice in their head that prepares them what to say next, rather than to the other person. Voss says it's important to shut out the voice in your head and you can do this by focusing only on what the other person is saying. By engaging in truly active listening, it disarms your counterpart by making them feel safe.

The goal of listening is to understand what counterparts need, for example, money or security. To find out what they need, it's important to make them feel safe and get them talking about what they want. Knowing what they want will help you discover what they need.

Voss says that the speed you talk and conduct the negotiations is extremely important. Slow it down, he says. All negotiators are prone to going too fast, which can make the counterpart feel like they're not being heard. This can undermine all hard-earned trust and rapport. Using a calm, deliberate voice is the most immediate and effective way of influencing the other person. The voice is a powerful tool in communication and can move a person's emotional state from one of high emotional arousal to one of peace and calm.

Voss describes three tones of voice for negotiations. These are:

- The late-night FM DJ voice. It's calm and slow and is made by inflecting the voice downwards. It was the voice he used in the bank robber hostage situation.

- The positive, playful voice. This should be your default voice, explains Voss. It suggests you are laid-back and friendly. It helps put you in a positive frame of mind. When you feel positive, you think quicker and influence the other person to feel positive. This makes them more likely to collaborate and problem solve rather than fight and resist. It allows you to be direct without causing offense.

- The direct and assertive voice. Voss says this is rarely used as it signals dominance and can make the other person become hostile.

Another important tool in negotiations is 'mirroring,' which helps bonding and building rapport by copying the speech patterns, the tone of voice, vocabulary, and body language of the other person. This works due to the instinctive fear that humans have of things that are different. We are naturally drawn to what is similar to us.

In negotiations, the negotiator should only focus on mirroring the words. The FBI negotiators mirror (in other words, repeat) the last three words or the three most important words that the counterpart has just said.

Research has shown how effective this can be. For example, one study found that waiters who repeated orders back to the customer received a 70% higher tip on average than the waiters who didn't.

Voss stresses that silence is an important part of the mirror technique. When you repeat the most important words back to the counterpart, adopt an inquisitive tone that suggests you are asking for help to understand what they mean. Then wait at least four seconds for the other person to think about what you said and form their reply.

Voss says the mirror technique takes practice to get used to and it can feel awkward in the beginning. However, it's valuable in almost any professional or social setting. He gives an example of who he considered to be a brilliant negotiator - Oprah Winfrey. She embraces the art of conversation and rapport (essential skills in negotiations) and got people talking on her talk show about all sorts of subjects, sometimes even against their best interests.

Chapter 3: Don't Feel Their Pain, Label it | How to Create Trust with Tactical Empathy

Voss starts by giving a real-life example of tactical empathy in action. In 1998, he was outside a high-rise apartment in Harlem. A group of fugitives had used automatic weapons in a shootout against a rival gang and now they were hiding in the locked apartment. Voss employed his late-night FM DJ voice and spoke to them about their fears, with statements such as, "it seems you don't want to come out" and "it looks like you don't want to get back to jail." For six hours, he repeated variations of these statements yet got no response. However, they eventually surrendered, saying it was Voss's voice and acknowledgment of their fears that made them feel calm enough to come out.

In traditional negotiations, the advice is to keep a poker face at all times, separate the people from the problem, and ignore emotions. However, a good negotiator, says Voss, should do the very opposite—they should identify and influence the emotions. Once they recognize the emotion, they should label it. This includes both their emotions and the emotions of others. The relationship between a negotiator and the counterpart is almost therapeutic, as the negotiator adopts a role similar to a psychotherapist who is gently prodding the patient to understand the problem. It involves talking less and listening more.

Tactical empathy involves paying attention to the other person by asking them how they are feeling and being determined to understand what's going on in their minds. It's to go beyond the surface feelings and work out how the emotional part of the brain is feeling. Voss stresses that it's not about being nice or agreeing with the other person. It's simply about understanding them and thinking about what makes sense to them.

Empathy is considered a soft communication skill, yet it also has a physical basis. By observing the face, tone of voice, and gestures of someone, our brain starts aligning with the other person in a process known as "neural resonance." This helps us better understand what the other person is thinking and feeling. A study at Princeton University found that good listeners who had engaged in neural resonance through listening, could anticipate what the speaker was about to say.

In the Harlem situation, Voss used tactical empathy to recognize and articulate the emotions of the fugitives. He calls this "labeling." Labeling verifies someone's emotions by acknowledging them. It exposes negative feelings and makes them seem less scary. By labeling an emotion, it moves it from system one to system two of our brains and helps us think rationally about what we are feeling. Good negotiators use subtle clues from the other person to identify their emotional state. This is the same way psychics work. Once the negotiator spots the emotion, they label it using statements or questions that use neutral prompts, such as "It seems..." or "It looks like..." Using "I think..." is too personal and makes the conversation about you. Labeling has two purposes—it can boost a good part of the negotiation, or it can diffuse a negative aspect.

Voss says that emotions have two parts: the first is "presenting behavior" which are the surface emotions you see and hear. The second is beneath the first and contains the underlying feelings that motivate behavior. A good negotiator needs to identify and label the underlying emotions in the second part. One way of doing this is to imagine you are in your counterpart's shoes. You may think the complete opposite of their beliefs and that's fine. What you're looking to do is to understand their situation and consider what they might be feeling beneath the surface.

A common mistake in dealing with emotions is to start a sentence with, "I don't mean to sound rude but..." and then hope whatever you say next will sound less harsh. However, the opposite happens—it gives those negative words credibility and makes them more real. Voss says the best way to approach this to change the process by using a tool called "accusation audit." This is when you list all the bad things the counterpart could say about you and then tell them these before they have a chance to say them. This has two benefits. First, it helps you identify their fears. Secondly, it shows empathy and that you understand how they are feeling. Also, the accusations can seem exaggerated when said aloud and it will make the counterpart more likely to seek a positive perspective.

Voss adds that tactical empathy is simply an extension of natural human interactions. It's not a fake conversation tool or a devious trick. It's actually about making better connections and creating meaningful relationships with others.

Chapter 4: Beware "yes" - Master "no" | How to Generate Momentum and Make it Safe to Reveal the Real Stakes

To explore the next negotiation skill, Voss sets a scene that most people will be familiar with—telemarketing. He describes how a typical telemarketer will ask a series of questions designed to lead the receiver down a route that encourages them to say "yes." However, pushing for a "yes," doesn't get the negotiation closer to a win. In fact, it can just make the receiver angry, frustrated, and desperate to say "no."

Voss says this typical selling technique supports the idea that "yes" is good, yet the role of "yes" and "no" is not as black and white as it seems. "No" isn't "anti-yes." Voss explains that in a good negotiation, getting a "no" is actually a good thing. It's an opportunity to remove what both parties don't want. Yet it's more than about figuring out what each side wants. Saying "no" makes the counterpart feel in control and safe. It's the start of the negotiation, not the end.

Voss gives an example with his teenage son. After he says "no" to whatever request his son has asked him, Voss becomes more open to hearing what his son has to say. By saying "no," it provides some initial protection and gives him space to then consider all the possibilities. Change can be scary and saying "no" avoids moving to a place that is different.

Saying "no" is a right we all have and in a negotiation, it's essential to give the counterpart that right from the very beginning. Once they've had the opportunity to say "no," then the negotiating environment becomes more collaborative and constructive. We have a deep human need for autonomy and to feel in control and saying "no" helps satisfy that need. When someone says "no," it rarely means that they have considered all the options and made a rational decision to reject the idea.

In fact, "no" generally doesn't mean rejection. It can mean the other side isn't ready to agree at that stage or is feeling uncomfortable with the situation. It could also mean they don't understand everything that's going on. They may feel they can't afford what you are offering, want something different, or want to talk over their decision with someone else before agreeing.

In contrast, "yes" doesn't always mean that the other person fully agrees with you. "yes" also isn't as clear as it may seem. There are three types

- Counterfeit: This is when the counterpart wants to reject your offer but says "yes" with a hidden agenda. This is either as a way of escaping the negotiation or to keep you talking to find out more information.

- Confirmation. This is a simple "yes" said out of reflex yet doesn't come with any promise of acting upon what was agreed.

- Commitment. This is the "yes" we are familiar with, the "yes" that means it's a true agreement.

Voss says all people are driven by two primitive impulses and those are to feel safe and secure and the need to feel in control. These deep-rooted urges come from the emotional part of the brain, known as system one. No matter how hard we try, we can't logically and rationally convince someone they are safe, secure, and in control. Instead, it's important to give them the opportunity to say "no" as this provides them with the security and autonomy they need. By saying "no," it calms system one down and reduces any extreme emotional responses. Once the person is in this zone, they are more willing to think rationally and be collaborative.

Saying "no" serves some important purposes in negotiations, both for the person saying it and the person receiving it. Hearing "no" allows the negotiator to slowly peel back the layers to discover what the real problem is and try to understand what the other person is thinking. For the person saying "no," it protects them from making ill-informed decisions as well as correcting any poor decisions that have already been made. It also buys them more time to think about the situation and consider the options.

It's good to begin the negotiation with a "no" as that sets up a constructive environment to continue. To get someone to say "no," you can mislabel their emotion which then invites them to correct you. Or, you can simply ask the counterpart what they don't want.

Chapter 5: Trigger the Two Words That Immediately Transform any Negotiation | How to Gain the Permission to Persuade

The Crisis Negotiation Unit (CNU) developed the Behavioral Change Stairway Model (BCSM). There are five stages of the BCSM: active listening, empathy, rapport, influence, and behavioral change. Voss says if you take someone through every stage of the model, it builds trust and empathy and eventually reaches the moment of "unconditional positive regard."

Unconditional positive regard is the basic acceptance and support of a person, no matter what that person says or does. Once this occurs, it opens the door to change. This is why it's so important in negotiations. If you can establish unconditional positive regard, the counterpart will be more willing to change their position. For most people, positive regard is conditional—we hide who we truly are, say what we think others want to hear or suppress what we really think in order to gain approval. This is why few social interactions result in actual behavioral change.

Voss says by using the BCSM, it can guide the counterpart to say the two most important words in a negotiation: "that's right." These two words break down any barriers between the two parties as it creates an understanding between them. It gives your counterpart the feeling that they have considered what you said and reached the conclusion that it's right on their own free will. People have a natural urge to participate in socially constructive behavior and the more they feel understood, the stronger that urge will be.

On the other hand, if they say "you're right," it's a sign of negotiations going wrong. When people say "you're right," it's often to get the other person to back off and leave them alone. It may mean that they agree with you, but they don't own the assumption.

Voss describes a hostage situation where "that's right" helped save the hostage's life. In 2000, Abu Sayyaf, a militant Islamic group, captured 24-year-old American traveler, Jeffrey Schilling. They requested a $10 million ransom for his safe release and as compensation for foreign war damages in the Philippines. Voss created a strategy to speak with the rebel leader, Abu Sabaya, through Benjie, the Philippine negotiator. His aim was for Sabaya to say, "That's right."

There were several listening tactics Voss used to help the negotiations. These included:

- Effective pauses to encourage conversation. Silence is powerful.

- Minimal encouragers, such as "yes" and "uh-huh" to signal that Benjie was paying full attention.

- Mirroring by listening to what Sabaya said and repeating the most important words back.

- Labeling by naming Sabaya's emotions, especially the ones relating to war damages as these were the most powerful.

- Paraphrasing by repeating what Sabaya said in Benjie's own words to show that he truly understands what's being said, rather than simply echoing the conversation.

- Summarize, which is a blend of paraphrasing and labeling the entire conversation.

These techniques got Sabaya to say, "That's right," and feel understood. This helped prevent Schilling's execution and gave him enough time to eventually escape unharmed.

Chapter 6: Bend Their Reality | How to Shape what is Fair

Voss explains that in a hostage situation involving the safe release of someone in exchange of a ransom, there is always leverage. Negotiation is never a linear formula and includes emotions and uncovered needs. This means it's possible to bend the reality of the hostage-takers to give them not what they think they deserve, but what the negotiator wants. This logic works in any negotiation.

In a hostage situation based on traditional negotiating logic, the best solution would be to split the ransom request and everyone leaves happy. However, this assumes a rational win-win mindset and it's highly likely that the hostage-takers have a win-lose approach. It's still important to build rapport and empathy but to be aware that splitting the difference can lead to undesirable outcomes. Voss says no deal is better than a bad one and points out that in a hostage situation, a bad deal is when the hostage-takers get the money and the hostage is killed.

Voss explains how time and deadlines are crucial elements in any negotiation. When the time is seemingly running out, it can make people do and say impulsive things that may be against their best interests. Deadlines can make us worry about a perceived loss in the future - for example, in business, if we miss a deadline, we may worry that our client will be angry and end the deal or our boss will be mad and we lose our chance of a promotion. In reality, deadlines are mostly subjective and almost always flexible. A good negotiator will resist the urge to succumb to deadline pressures and use its power to influence the other party.

The term "fair" is an important concept in negotiation. If people feel they have been treated fairly, they tend to respect agreements. If they feel they have been disrespected, they will resist. Voss highlights the importance of this concept with an example of the "proposer and accepter" game. The proposer is given $10 to split between himself and the accepter. If the accepter refuses the offer, the $10 is returned to Voss. The results show that any offer less than half ($5 each) is usually rejected. If it's less than a quarter (offering the accepter $2 or less) the accepter is insulted and will more than likely turn the offer down. What this shows is that emotions play a role in our decision-making. If we considered this offer rationally, receiving even $1 is better than nothing. However, due to the perceived unfairness of the situation, we would normally prefer for both to walk away with nothing rather than get $1 and the proposer leaving with $9.

Fairness can be used to build strong and positive negotiations. Starting the negotiation by saying you want what's fair for the other person and inviting them to interrupt at any moment they feel badly treated, sets the scene for an empathetic and open exchange.

The way you present an offer can change your counterpart's perspective. This is known as "bending reality." For example, if someone offers you $20 to do three minutes of work, then you may calculate this as the equivalent of $400 per hour and see it as a great offer. However, if you find out later that the three minutes of work made one million dollars for the other person, you may feel outraged and want more. How an offer is framed will influence the reaction of the other person.

Decision-making is irrational yet it still has consistent patterns. A way of understanding these rules is through a concept called "prospect theory." This explains how people choose between options that involve risk and says that people prefer certainty rather than probabilities, even when the probability offers a better choice. This is known as the "certainty effect." It links to a concept called "loss aversion," which describes how people will take greater risks to avoid losses than to achieve gains.

Loss aversion is an important part of negotiation. Negotiators can use it to persuade a counterpart that they have something to lose if the deal falls through. There are several techniques to use the loss aversion concept in negotiations. These are:

- Anchor their emotions by using empathy and an accusation audit. An accusation audit is a powerful tool as it prompts the feelings of potential loss and gets the counterpart ready to avoid a loss at all costs.

- When negotiating monetary clauses, allow the other side to have their say first. The first price is almost always negotiable so be prepared to oppose the offer.

- If you have no other choice but to go first when negotiating money, use this as an opportunity to establish a range between two figures.

- Complement monetary terms with non-monetary offers. It can make money negotiations seem more reasonable and the non-monetary offer could be highly desirable for the counterpart. For example, Voss describes a hostage situation in Haiti where the hostage-takers demanded $150,000 for the life of a hostage. Eventually, they agreed to take less than $5,000 after the nephew of the hostage offered a new car stereo along with the ransom.

- Using odd numbers in monetary negotiations has a strong psychological effect. Numbers ending in '0' tend to feel like temporary numbers that are open to negotiation. Numbers that are precise and haven't been rounded up or down seem more permanent.

- Offering a gift can have a powerful effect in negotiation as it opens up the ingrained "reciprocity" behavior in people. When we receive a gift or kindness, we tend to feel obliged to repay the debt.

These negotiation techniques can be applied to getting a better salary. Voss recommends starting by being persistent in asking for non-salary terms—this may lead to a counter-offer of more money.

Chapter 7: Create the Illusion of Control | How to Calibrate Questions to Transform Conflict into Collaboration

Voss describes a hostage situation that was a disaster. In 2001, Abu Sayyaf kidnapped 20 hostages in Manila, including three Americans. The negotiation was shrouded in mistakes, especially communication issues. The U.S. forces were unable to communicate with the rebel leaders in order to kickstart the negotiations. The Philippine government and army declared outright war on the terrorist group that led to further confusion. It ended in several hostages being killed, including two of the American captives.

Upon reflection, Voss says their negotiation strategy was based on a retaliation mindset where the U.S. forces would demand something from the rebels and would be faced with a demand right back at them. Their approach was based on overcoming the rebel leaders and defeating them, rather than collaborating and cooperating. This paralyzed the conversation between the two parties as both wanted something from the other but refused to give anything back. The FBI never asked for proof of life, as they were worried this would trigger the "reciprocity rule" where they would then be in debt to Abu Sayyaf.

What would have promoted a better conversation are open-ended questions or "calibrated" questions that introduce ideas in a calm and cooperative way.

Psychologist Kevin Dulton, described a concept called an "unbelief," which is an active resistance to what the other person is saying and results in a complete rejection. It leads to a standoff where each side imposes their perspective on the other. In order to create a collaborative and constructive setting, it's vital that the other side lets go of their "unbelief." This doesn't mean they start to believe what the negotiator says; rather, it means they stop disbelieving the negotiator. The way to do this is to use calibrated questions.

Calibrated questions give the counterpart an illusion of control. To effectively use calibrated questions, start by deciding the direction you want the conversation to go and what outcome you want to achieve. Then design calibrated questions that deliberately guide the discussion. Calibrated questions are worded in a way that makes them seem like a request for help, rather than an accusation or a put-down. They use soft phrases, such as "perhaps," "maybe," and "it seems," which take the aggression out of a potentially confrontational statement. They also avoid close-ended questions that only invite a "yes" or "no" answer. Instead, they opt for reporter-style questions that prompt longer responses, especially questions beginning with "what" and "how."

In negotiations, use calibrated questions early and often. This helps you learn more about your counterpart and gather plenty of information about them and the negotiation. These types of questions work because they show that you want the same thing as the other person but you need them to help you overcome the problem. This is especially effective when your counterpart is naturally egotistical or aggressive. They make the counterpart feel they are in charge, but really, it's you that's framing the conversation.

In order to work, Voss says that self-control and emotional regulation are critical variables of calibrated questions. The way you frame the questions and the tone of voice you use are crucial in delivering the questions in an open and honest way. If you are reacting emotionally, the questions can come across as aggressive. It's important to learn how to remain rational in a negotiation. To do this, pause and think before saying anything. This gives you time to collect your thoughts and stop any knee-jerk, impulsive reactions. If your counterpart verbally abuses you, don't jump in with a counterattack. Instead, take a pause and ask a calibrated question that challenges the abuse in an inquisitive, understanding way.

The feeling of not being in control makes us adopt a type of behavior called a "hostage mentality." This is when we react to a lack of power and control by becoming defensive, resisting, and fighting back. The fight or flight defense mechanism kicks in and our limbic part of the brain (the emotional part) overwhelm our rational thinking. This leads to extreme emotional and impulsive reactions. Whenever this happens in a negotiation, it will always end in a negative result.

Chapter 8: Guarantee Execution | How to Spot the Liars and Ensure Follow-Through from Everyone Else

Even the best negotiation strategy in the world can go wrong if it's not executed properly. This is one of the lessons Voss teaches in this chapter. He starts with an example of a prison siege in Louisiana, in which a handful of inmates took the warden and some staff hostage and were threatening them with knives. What made it worse was the prisoners were tense and disorganized, so emotions were running high. It was clear that they'd had enough and wanted this hostage situation to end. However, they were afraid of being physically punished by the guards if they surrendered.

Voss made a plan to give one inmate a walkie-talkie, take him back to the jail, and he would then call to the others to say he got back fine without being beaten up. Everything went well until one member of the SWAT team, who didn't know the master plan, confiscated the walkie-talkie. The lack of news from the inmate sent the other prisoners into a panic and they threatened to cut off one of the hostage's fingers. However, Voss managed to get the walkie-talkie quickly delivered to the jailed inmate and the hostage situation was resolved.

Voss stresses that a "yes" (an agreement) isn't worth anything without a "how" (implementation). He gives another example of an American tour guide, Jose, who was kidnapped in the Ecuadorian jungle by Colombian rebels. The FBI communicated with the rebels through Julie, Jose's wife, and insisted she respond to every demand with a question asking how she could meet that demand. This bought time while the rebels contemplated how they could respond to her questions. The delays in considering how to answer Julie's "how" meant that they let their guard down and Jose was able to safely escape.

Voss calls these types of questions "calibrated questions" and they are designed to keep the conversation going and to get the counterpart to actively participate in your problem-solving. Voss refers to it as a gentle "no" as it doesn't reject the counterpart's offer directly, yet still manages to deny the demand. For example, when the rebels requested $5 million for Jose, Julie replied, "how am I supposed to do that?" It doesn't explicitly say "no" but it subtly signals her position. The tone of voice when saying this is critical—it must be inquisitive, like a request for help. This creates a kind of "forced empathy." If it's said too harshly, it can appear accusing.

The benefit of using "how" in negotiations is it makes the counterpart express the implementation themselves, which makes them feel they own the conclusion. This is important as people make more effort to carry out an idea when they feel it's theirs. If after using calibrated questions, the counterpart responds with either "you're right" or "I'll try," this means they don't yet truly believe they own the solution. In this case, keep asking calibrated questions until they are able to define the implementation in their own words. A deal is nothing without implementation so this stage of the negotiation is vital.

Voss also mentions the importance of being aware that the negotiation could be beyond just you and your counterpart. There could be other agents "behind the negotiation table" that can exert their influence on the counterpart and change the direction of the exchange. You can found out about potential others by asking calibrated questions that aim to draw out information about who will be affected by these decisions.

Body language is one of the most important parts of negotiations, says Voss. Albert Mehrabian, a psychology professor, created the 7-38-55 rule. This refers to how much a person interprets a message—7% is based on words, 38% on the tone of voice, and 55% on the body language and facial gestures. You can use this to your advantage to detect if someone is lying. Pay attention to the tone of voice and body language and whether these match to the meanings of the words being said. If it doesn't, there is a good possibility the speaker is lying.

Voss discusses the "counterfeit yes," which is when someone says "yes" with the hidden intention of not committing to that agreement. The way to avoid getting a counterfeit "yes" is by using the "Rule of Three." This gets the person saying the same thing three times and thus tripling its strength. The most successful way to get someone to say "yes" three times is to use different tactics to draw out the agreement, such as a combination of labeling, summarizing, and calibrated questions.

There are also techniques to detect lies at the negotiation table. One of these is the "Pinocchio Effect." This is the tendency of liars to speak with more complex sentences to try to win over the suspicious counterpart. The long words and long sentences are likened to Pinocchio's long nose when he lies. Liars also tend to use more third-person pronouns and avoid using "I" as it puts distance between them and the lie.

Voss gives a tip on how to identify the importance or position of a person and gauge how much power and influence they have in the decision-making process. The more they use personal pronouns such as "I," "me," and "my," the less important they tend to be. If they use more third-person pronouns such as "they" or "we," "we" means they probably hold an important position and use these pronouns to avoid being cornered when it comes to making a final decision.

Chapter 9: Bargain Hard | How to Get Your Price

All of the techniques learned over the last few chapters such as mirroring, labeling, and accusation audits lead to one final step—the bargaining part of the negotiation. This is the part that most people feel the most uncomfortable about.

Voss says that to bargain well, it's vital to eliminate all your assumptions about what the bargaining process is and instead learn to recognize subtle psychological clues. These are the strategies and roles people adopt at the negotiating table. The better you can read them, the more likely you can participate in a successful negotiation.

Everyone has their own personal negotiating style. This is formed through our experiences from childhood up to the present day with influence coming from teachers, parents, culture, work environment, and many other factors. Knowing your own negotiating style helps you leverage your strengths and recognize your weaknesses. It also helps you identify the style of your counterpart and tweak your strategy and mindset accordingly to set the conditions for flowing, collaborative communication. There are three main categories—analysts, accommodators, and assertive. To be a truly effective communicator, it's good to be able to use the characteristics of all three when circumstances demand it.

Analysis

Analyst styles approach negotiating calmly, methodically, and thoroughly. The most important thing for them is to get the best result possible in a systematic way that minimizes all mistakes—even if this means it takes them longer than expected. They stick to their goals and like working independently. When they speak, they naturally adopt the late-night FM DJ voice, yet it may sound cold and unapproachable, rather than calming. They pay close attention to details and arrive at negotiations well prepared. Reciprocity is important to them and if they don't receive something back from a counterpart, the analyst style will lose their trust in them. If an analyst remains silent, they are probably not angry; they are just thinking about the situation. Voss says if this sounds like you, smiling more throughout the negotiation and employing more positive body language can help build a better rapport.

Accommodator

The accommodator style loves to accommodate their counterpart and their ideal outcome is a win-win situation. Flowing communication means a lot to them and they want to build a strong relationship with their counterpart. This style is the most likely to develop a great rapport but struggle to implement anything from the discussion. They want to understand their counterpart and find it easy to build empathy with their friendly, pleasant voices. If you are faced with an accommodator style, it may be hard to find their real objectives. This is because they tend to brush over problematic issues in an attempt to avoid conflict. Calibrated questions can help bring these objectives to the surface, as well as putting the accommodator's talk into action.

Assertive

The assertive type sees time as money and judges their performance on how many things they can accomplish in a period of time. They are fiery, direct, and love winning. Their communication style can be described as aggressive and they focus on getting the job done. They value being heard and will only listen to the point of views of others once they feel their perspective has been listened to and understood. If you're dealing with an assertive type, there are several tools which are effective to show you are listening, such as mirroring, labeling, summarizing, and calibrated questions. Their focus is on their own goals rather than the objectives of others. Unlike the analyst style which sees silence as a moment to think or the accommodator who believes silence means the other person is angry, the assertive type sees silence as an opportunity to talk more.

It's essential to understand your counterpart in order to bargain effectively. Voss recommends not treating others the way you want to be treated. Instead, treat them the way they want to be treated.

If you feel the negotiation is going nowhere, there are some techniques to shake up the exchange and assert yourself. Voss suggests using a hint of well-timed anger to signal that you are unimpressed with a poor deal. Using the pronoun "I" is also a useful way to set boundaries without running into a full-blown confrontation. Adopting a "ready to walk" mindset prevents you from being trapped by a bad deal and gives you the confidence to push for what you want. Never resort to personal attacks and avoid seeing your counterpart as the enemy. Even when you're using these tactics to set limits, you should always aim for a collaborative, empathetic, and constructive relationship.

Finally, Voss introduces the "Ackerman Bargaining" model. This is a model for offering a counteroffer in a negotiation. It begins by setting a target price. For example, you want to negotiate your rent as your landlord is asking for expensive monthly installments. Your ideal price is $1,000 per month. This becomes your target price. Then set the first offer at 65% of your target price. For example, you offer to your landlord $650 per month. When they refuse the first offer, you offer a further three incremental increases of 85%, 95%, and finally 100% (in this case, $850, $950, and then your ideal price of $1,000). When you get to the final price, adjust it slightly to give a precise figure, such as $9,967. Once you have given that final figure, offer a non-monetary item to make the deal more attractive.

Chapter 10: Find the Black Swan | How to Create Breakthroughs by Revealing the Unknown Unknowns

In this chapter, Voss introduces a concept that can completely change the game of a negotiation—the black swans. Before describing what they are, he begins with an incident on June 17, 1981 when William Griffin held nine bank employees hostage in Rochester. Prior to arriving at the bank, he had shot and killed two people, including his mother, and injured several more. For three and a half hours, he fired more than 100 rounds from his shotgun at the police. During this time, he demanded that the police shoot him before 3 pm; otherwise, he would kill a hostage.

The police knew that hostage-takers never meet deadlines and there is always room to negotiate so they didn't react. When 3 pm came, they saw one of the hostages, Margaret Moore, move towards the glass doors of the bank entrance. Once she stopped, Griffin fired two rounds into her back, sending her flying through the glass. He walked towards the entrance where snipers finally killed him. This situation became known as the "suicide by cop" phenomenon, where an individual creates a horrific situation in order to be killed by the police.

The main issue with this case was that it went against every hostage situation the police were used to. They tried to fit this new information into the frameworks created based on past hostage experiences. They believed that all hostage-takers wanted something such as monetary compensation or recognition for something. They never expected that this man wanted a police-assisted suicide. These expectations led the police to overlook the fact that something about this case was different. For example, hostage-takers always have demands, yet Griffin didn't. The nearby murders also showed he was capable of killing people without any demands being met.

It's these unknowns that Voss refers to as '"black swans." They are things that happen that we previously thought either were impossible or had simply never imagined. It's anything unknown that can dramatically change the course of the negotiation. They indicate that basing judgments on past experience doesn't always lead to the most accurate predictions.

In every negotiation, there are three types of information. There are the "known knowns" which is the information we clearly know about, such as the counterpart's name, their offer, and our past experiences. There are the "known unknowns" which are the things we know exist but we are unsure of. For example, a counterpart may be replaced by another counterpart halfway through negotiations. And finally, there are the things that we don't know that we don't know. They are game-changing factors yet we would never have imagined them. Voss gives the example of a counterpart wanting a deal to fail as they are moving to a competitor.

When things don't feel quite right, it's often because we haven't considered the unknown unknowns. We are basing our assumptions on known knowns which have a role in guiding us but can often blind us too. Voss recommends approaching each negotiation with the mindset that there are at least three black swans on the table. It takes the right line of questioning to reveal them (calibrated questions are useful here). They may not seem that important to the counterpart, yet once you know what they are, it can completely change the negotiation direction.

Voss says black swans are useful in negotiations due to the leverage they bring. Leverage is important as it influences the status quo of the deal. The more a person feels they have to lose, the less leverage they have. There are three   types   of   leverage:

- Positive leverage. This is the ability of the negotiator to give the counterpart what they want or need. If a counterpart says, "I want..." and refers to your offer, you have positive leverage.

- Negative leverage. This is the ability of the negotiator to make the counterpart suffer by applying the loss aversion principle. It's important not to overdo negative leverage as it may be perceived as taking away the counterpart's autonomy. If this happens, discussions are more than likely to break down.

- Normative leverage. This is when the negotiator uses their counterpart's set of norms and morals to their advantage. The negotiator can highlight discrepancies between the counterpart's beliefs and their actions to encourage them to rethink their position.

One way of activating normative leverage is to understand the counterpart's religion, as this tends to influence their behavior. Other ways to get people to trust you and make it easier to find the black swan is using the similarity principle. This refers to the fact that we tend to trust and like people more when we see them as similar to us. This can be anything from race and nationality to something more subtle such as similar dress sense and associations with the same sports club.

Voss says that it's human nature to fear the unknown. We tend to ignore, avoid, or label situations or people that make us afraid. A common expression for labeling unknown behavior is to say, "They're crazy." When we say that, that's often the best moment to find the black swan. This is the moment when we see or hear something that doesn't make sense to us, which is a sign that it is beyond our known knowns.

It's common for a negotiator to think their counterpart is crazy yet there are several underlying reasons for that. It could be that the counterpart is ill-informed and doesn't have the right information to make a good decision. If someone is using incomplete facts, they may appear irrational to those who have more information. It could also be that the counterpart is constrained yet doesn't want to reveal this. For example, they may want to purchase something yet don't have the budget and are embarrassed to admit it. Finally, they may have other interests. For example, William Griffin was interested in a cop-assisted suicide, not in monetary demands.

To uncover black swans, it's best to do this face-to-face. Also, look for clues during informal situations when people have their guard down, as this can be the most revealing. During structured meetings or formal encounters, your counterpart will more likely be guarded and deliberately hiding vital clues.

Voss finishes by reminding the reader that pushing for what you want is not selfish or bullying. Sincere, genuine conflict is a good thing as it stimulates problem-solving and pushes us towards achieving our goals. Rather than avoid conflict, try approaching negotiations with the idea that honest conflict can be used to create a collaborative and empathetic setting.

Quiz

For all readers who like the book and want to put their knowledge to the test, this quiz is what they need. Questions are easy to answer and every answer can be found within the "summary" and "quiz answers" sections. So let's get started.

QUESTION 1

Why is saying "no" almost always good when it comes to negotiation?

A) By saying "no" we immediately show who is 'in charge' of the entire situation.

B) When both sides say "no" they show that they share disagreements in similar areas of negotiation.

C) Saying "no" is necessary because by giving affirmative answers to every demand will show that we are can be manipulated.

D) Everything above.

QUESTION 2

New information, something that can greatly impact the "flow" of the negotiation process, something that was not known before is called a...

A) ...Black Frog.

B) ...Black Fish.

C) ...Black Swan.

D) ...Black Stork.

QUESTION 3

"Assertive and analytical negotiators are contradictory to one another."

A) TRUE

B) FALSE

QUESTION 4

"_____negotiators tend to speak in friendly manner and when they speak they often speak about certain things, which are

unconnected to _____.
Their main goal is to ensure _____
and _____ relationship with
the other side."

QUESTION 5

Why is beneficial for every good negotiator to practice empathy?

A) Because empathy shows us that we care for other side.

B) By being empathetic, we are able to see how other side feels and thus react accordingly.

C) By being empathetic, we can feel how other side feels but remain at the 'same side' where we are.

D) Everything above.

QUESTION 6

"When we actively listen to someone, that someone will see that their demands are acknowledged and respected."

A) TRUE

B) FALSE

ANSWERS

QUESTION 1 – B

QUESTION 2 – C

QUESTION 3 – TRUE

QUESTION 4 – "accommodative, the negotiation process, positive, friendly."

QUESTION 5 – C

QUESTION 6 – TRUE

CONCLUSION

For every reader who wanted a book about negotiation and how to lead a negotiation with the maximum chance for success, *Never Split the Difference* is just the right read. It is a book written by Chris Voss, an expert in negotiations, together with Tahl Raz, a writer for the *New York Journal.*

Reading this book is like reading top secret confidential documents. It is filled with thrill and the reader never knows what they will find out by reading the next page. The thing I liked most about the book is how the author, although an expert in his field regarding negotiation, uses language that is easy to understand for every reader. Sure, there are certain parts of the book which contain some harder to understand terminology, but that is minimal. The book is written so that almost everyone who is interested in how to get the best when doing a negotiation will be able to understand.

Never Split the Difference is divided into several chapters. In every part of the book, Voss explains a certain aspect of the negotiation process. All the parts together form a perfect whole, which looks great, but readers do not necessarily need to read every single part to get a firm grasp on what the book is about. Every part has something that the previous parts did not have and every part opens a new window into the negotiation process.

And when it comes to a negotiation, there are many aspects and many things to learn. That is why Voss speaks of the importance of active listening to the other side, empathy (but not sympathy), the importance of saying "yes" and "no" at the right times, different types of negotiators, and something that he calls the "Black Swan." This is something that I liked a lot. The Black Swan can be anything that influences the course of the negotiation process – something that both sides did not know prior to the beginning of the negotiation, but when they find out, it will definitely impact the flow of negotiation or can even terminate it.

Educational, easy-to-read, written in professional manner, but with a minimal use of complicated terminology, *Never Split the Difference* is a book that every good negotiator or any person who want to be a good negotiator should definitely read. It contains many facts and things that many of us probably did not know, but that can greatly influence how our negotiations proceed in the future.

I definitely recommend reading this book. Many readers will find it so interesting and educational that they will want to read it a second time. *Never Split the Difference* is a book for both professional and everyday use.

Thank You and more...

Thank you for taking your time to read this book, I hope now you hold a greater knowledge about Never Split the Difference.

Before you go, would you mind leaving us a review where you purchased your book?

It will mean a lot to us, and help us continue making more summaries for you and for others.

Thank you once again!

Yours warmly,

FURTHER READINGS

If you are interested in other self-help summary books. Click the link below.

1- Summary of Atomic Habits by Speed-Summary

https://www.amazon.com/dp/B07RBT6ZBG/

2- Summary of Dr. Gundry Diet Evolution by Speed-Summary

https://www.amazon.com/dp/B07RL831SC/

3- Summary of The Obesity Code by Speed-Summary

https://www.amazon.com/dp/B07RSN3ZJP/

You can click the link below or just search Speed-Summary on Amazon.

https://www.amazon.com/s?i=digital-
text&rh=p_27%3ASpeed-
Summary&s=relevancerank&text=Speed-
Summary&ref=dp_byline_sr_ebooks_1

Made in the USA
San Bernardino, CA
24 March 2020